SCHAPIRO'S MODIFIED RULES OF GOLF FOR SENIORS

Randall T. Schapiro, M.D., FAAN

Illustrated by Timothy Gaffney

Copyright ©2023 Randall Schapiro

All rights reserved.

ISBN: 9798362769093

This book is subject to the condition that no part of this book is to be reproduced, transmitted in any form or means; electronic or mechanical, stored in a retrieval system, photocopied, recorded, scanned, or otherwise. Any of these actions require the proper written permission of the author.

DEDICATION

To all senior golfers who play for fun and their spouses who put up with them.

And off we go! Golf and retirement go hand-in-hand.

TABLE OF CONTENTS

INTRODUCTION 1

WHY GOLF AS A SENIOR 4

PICKING THE PROPER TEE BOX FOR SENIORS 8

MODIFYING THE RULES 11

BETTER LUCKY THAN GOOD 24

MANNERS 29

APPENDIX 33

ABOUT THE AUTHOR AND ILLUSTRATOR 34

INTRODUCTION

Just who is this guy Schapiro? And what does he know about golf rules? Just for the record, I am a nobody when it comes to golf. I am an old guy in my upper seventies and did not play golf as a youth. I took it up in my sixties. I have scanned the *Rules of Golf* several times but have never actually read it and probably never will.

I never had the time to golf, but now that I'm retired, I've decided to take it up for "social reasons". Meaning I have a different perspective from that of a long-time, seasoned golfer. For me, it's a different game than for a "real" or professional golfer.

I learned right away that there is only one prevailing reason to play golf, especially for seniors who are not professional-level golfers. That reason is to have FUN, and that attitude must prevail throughout the round. I will come back to that over and over: have FUN! There are times on the golf course that…, anyway, FUN is the answer! However, to have fun and not be continually embarrassed, you must have a certain amount of skill to play.

To gain that skill at a senior age means lessons from a real professional golfer or instructor. There probably is no other way around that. A seasoned ski instructor once told me that, *at some point, there is no substitute for putting some miles on the boards.* This logic applies to learning senior golf as well. There is no substitute to playing without taking lessons, but not initially. Along with that, there is no substitute for practice, whether on the driving range, putting surface, or on the course! However, you do not want to leave your game out on the driving range! At our age, we have only so many swings left, so use them wisely! All this takes time, but we are retired and have the time.

We also need the wherewithal, as golf can be quite expensive. To get started, there are many stores that sell used clubs which still have a few strokes left in them. There are also many golf courses with reasonable fees, so there is little excuse not to get your game up and running!

This brings us to what is the best way to turn a game of skill into a game of fun (and skill). Now, after many years of having fun, I want to share my experience, knowing that many will simply laugh and/or cry about how my advice is not the right way to play golf and that any other way is simply stupid or wrong. You know, they may be right, but frankly, I don't care.

WHY GOLF AS A SENIOR

Why should a senior take up a sport like golf? I already answered this: to have FUN! However, there are other reasons to play which are also (but not equally) important. Here are my reasons why you should play golf as a senior.

1. First and foremost, **to have FUN**.
2. I love competition and want to beat my golf buddies into submission. If that is your goal, stop reading, as much that follows does not apply to you! Competition here is with yourself, gaining self-improvement over time. Don't pay attention to your buddies and their abilities.
3. Golf gets you out of the house and about the town and maybe breathe the air (depending on where you live, some places you need to see the air to breathe it).

4. Exercise is important. Driving around in a golf cart is hardly exercise, but it is certainly better than not doing it. If you can walk the course, **wow** for you!
5. It takes around four hours to play. When working, it sounds like a lot of time, maybe impossible. However, once retired, it sounds like a great filler of time. What can be better than filling time with a fun activity that allows you to be outside and moving!?
6. We all have tempers, some greater than others. There's nothing quite like venting your frustration at a golf ball to help you calm down! Sometimes all you need is a good shout (or even a swear word) to help you let off some steam. To my knowledge, golf balls do not talk back and do not attack the person hitting them. So, let it all out, and then get over it and move on. Only a few people will think you're crazy. But honestly, it doesn't matter. They're crazy as well.
7. The social part of golf is especially important. You get to "know" the people

you play golf with. Social interaction is essential to seniors who no longer have the work environment to socialize within. You all, coming from different walks of life, have something in common: golf. You can talk for hours about that, exaggerating each shot, and bragging about your accomplishments on the course.
8. Now that you are a golfer, watching golf on TV is much more fun! You can relate to each professional shot and sometimes actually believe that you would've made that shot. Of course, that is imagination at work, but you can believe it. Golf is not only a great time filler but also a fun one.
9. Golfing opens up significant gift opportunities. There is always something a golfer needs: from essentials such as balls, clubs, tees to towels, golfing aids, gift certificates for tee times, and much more. There is a plethora of things to buy, give, and have FUN with!
10. You may or may not want to keep score. That can depend on how the day is going

but in general, keeping your score (privately) allows you to see your progress over time. You can compete with yourself.

11. If, sadly, you are a person who likes to compete with others on the course, go ahead and golf with someone else who wants to compete – and have FUN doing it!
12. When on the golf course and concentrating on each shot, stop and look around at the beauty of the landscape. Golf courses are usually beautifully designed and should be admired!
13. Dress for success! Most courses require a certain outfit in sartorial splendor! So, embrace the beauty. With a nice shirt, golf shorts, or slacks, be ready to show off!

PICKING THE PROPER TEE BOX FOR SENIORS

Somewhere along the line, golf courses developed color codes and the naming of tee boxes. While some have modernized, most naming is done in a sexist way to no advantage of seniors who have lost their way. We (men and women) do not have to accept the idea that red tees are restricted to ladies.

This means we must look beyond the scorecard to find the right place to tee off to have the most FUN. The forward tees should no longer be named the "ladies' tees". Obviously, they are the forward tees and simply that. Ladies who are very good golfers may want to move back to complement their skills.

Seniors (and others) can play from whatever tee box they choose, depending on how far they hit their tee shot. There should be no embarrassment to moving forward if that is what it takes to put the ball in play and achieve the senior goal, a bogey (senior par) on the hole.

For most of us (guys and gals), that means forward. I know egos step in because we have been programmed to think that we need to be female to golf from the forward tees, but hey, get over it. This way, couples play from the same tee box, and that can make it easier to argue with each other in a timely fashion. When seniors step up to the first tee, there may initially be a hesitation: should I or shouldn't I move up to where I will have the most fun? Move up! It will speed up play, and all will be happier.

If you are younger, long, and lanky, and want to show off, move back, but you likely will not have as much fun to show for your ego. We can follow the ball easier because we are closer to where it will land!

Serious golfers reading this are likely to be seething because we hackers may be finding our scores easier to lower, and they will find it unfair. I ask, "unfair to whom?" Certainly not to me, so I really do not care if they feel that way.

So, off we go to the first tee box from the front tee. Here's hoping that it's copper or any color other than red because red appears to be reserved for the ladies, and we are genderless in this endeavor.

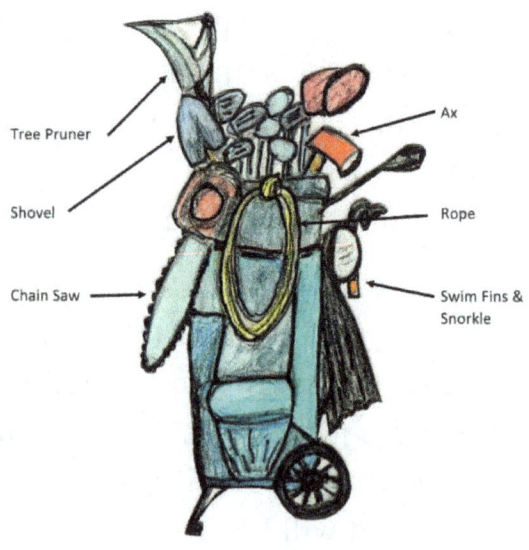

A well-equipped bag for playing Schapiro's modified rules of golf.

MODIFYING THE RULES

I recognize that in competitions, it is essential to have strict rules to determine the winner fairly. However, in recreational, senior golfing, each person should compete with themselves, not their partner. Golfers, particularly male golfers, who have golfed for years sometimes appear bored with the game and need to add enticements to get through the round.

This can involve betting, competing on each hole, getting closer to the pin, etc. It's enough to hit the ball, for many of us, without adding the stress of competition. Every golfer has learned that the harder they try to hit the ball and the farther they try to hit the ball, the worse the shot becomes.

Overthinking each shot is counter-productive and slows the game down significantly. Competition will lead to guaranteed frustration for you and all those around you! If you need competition like this, golf with golfers who want it but don't mix with those of us whose goals are different altogether.

With this in mind, step up to the first tee, the forward one, and begin the FUN!

Oops, the ball shanked. Under the modified rules, that shot is not counted, and a "breakfast" ball appears. Always step to the tee with an extra ball (or two) in your pocket and produce it when needed. If that hooks, maybe a Mulligan is necessary. It is the first tee, and jitters are normal. No big deal, just do it.

The driving range is not unusual to be adjacent to the first tee. Be aware of the color of the driving range balls. If they are yellow, use a white ball on the first tee. If the driving range balls are white, consider a yellow ball because you may be chasing it into a sea of balls that look alike unless you've used a different color. After that, it does not matter what color you have. Just have FUN.

After the first tee shot, we are off and running. If the ball found its way into a fairway bunker, make a decision based on how you feel

Time For a Breakfast Ball.

that day. It is totally okay with Schapiro's modified rules of golf to remove the ball from the bunker with your hands, feet, or rake and place it on the fairway to give the best advantage with the second shot.

[You have NOT lost a stroke with that maneuver, you just made a smart move].

If you feel you are up to the bunker challenge, take it but don't say you were not warned. You do not want to start your game on the wrong foot.

If there is a tree in the way to the green, there are a couple of choices for the senior golfer. One is to cut the tree down. Carrying a chainsaw makes the bag heavier, but it may come in handy. Alternatively, moving the ball away from the tree is quite reasonable and allowed. Hitting the tree may constitute a "do-over", depending on where the ball lands. Unfortunately, many balls are lost after they hit a tree. This is because the tree eats them to grow stronger. A drop may be necessary, and because the tree is at fault, there is no penalty.

As we approach the second shot, we should review some of the rules of the Schapiro Modified Scoring System. The first is to keep your own score, preferably privately. Since some cheating will inevitably occur, keep it private. It is your score to do as you wish. You are cheating yourself, hurting no one else. [This does not apply if you are trying to develop a handicap for competition with others]. But my point here is to make this a contest with just yourself. And to have some FUN.

There are some general modified rules you may want to follow:

1. If the lie is bad, change it. Make it as playable as necessary to achieve a decent potential shot. Remember, this is about having fun, not torturing yourself.
2. If the rough is too long or too rocky, move the ball. Long roughs simply mean that they were too busy to mow, and no penalty should be assessed. If too rocky, damage to the golf club may occur, which is not cost-effective, so a change is necessary. You did not put the rocks there, so you should not be penalized!
3. Sand on the course can be challenging or may be grossly unfair. Sand is the term, but often dirt is the reality. Sand bunkers

can appear to have a golf ball magnet in them.

Be Sure to Set Your Brakes Fully!

Depending on the conditions, there may or may not be a fair shot out of them. Take a shot or two and if successful, do a dance. But if not, throw the ball out, and count it as one stroke. Don't ruin the hole by getting frustrated on several miss-hits. If the lip to the bunker is not great, an aggressive putt with a putter can give amazing results for those of us who cannot control our sand wedge shot.
4. Dealing with trees was already specified. Ball movement is recommended, but a chainsaw is an option.

I knew I shudda packed that chain saw ...

5. Play "Ready, golf." Get to the ball as efficiently as possible, and if ready, golf. Waiting for golfers looking for a ball or figuring out a strategy only slows play.

Move along, and everyone will be happier. If you find you are losing many balls, simply buy cheaper ones.
6. There will be bad holes, no matter how good a golfer you may be. If you are going to be three over par on any hole, consider packing up and moving along. The worst you can do on any hole under this system is three over par, so give up when appropriate. Save your energy for the next hole. You may need it!
7. There is nothing in this system that says you need to keep score. The goal is FUN and if scoring impedes this goal, simply don't.
8. Water on a golf course may not be there to drink. The ball may feel it needs a drink and find its way to the water for a dip. Did you put the water there? No! If your ball is not disciplined appropriately and finds its way into the lake or stream, drop a new ball away from the water and consider the stroke taken to get there as penalty enough. Remember to carry a ball retriever to fish for golf balls. You will catch more of them

than fishing for fish in a lake! However, use the ball retriever with skill. Falling into the lake may ruin a good game, but it may be a good idea on a hot day. Driving the cart close to the water may result in a fine necessitated by dragging the cart out of the water.

9. Unless it really bothers you, leave the flagpole in on the greens. It slows play to pull and replace the pole 18 times. If the ball bounces off the pole because there is not enough space between the pole and the outside of the hole, give yourself credit for the putt. It would have been good, if not for the pole.

10. If you are within three feet or so of the hole, move along with the "gimmee." You know you are automatic from 10 feet out, so a three or six-footer is no big deal. Simply announce the "gimmee" putt (or not) and take credit as a make.

11. Birdies are fun and rare but remember to bury the duck or coot; otherwise, the

coyotes will get them! Hitting a goose does not count because they are such a big target. Hitting a "provisional" is always wise, as the second shot is usually better than the first. Simply substitute the shots taking the better of the two.

An alternative to the "Gimmee," Putting Rule.

We are all "second team all Americans," and are raised being told to "take your best shot." The worst of the two was simply a practice shot, and practice is supposed to make perfect. Taking more than two shots is

an overload and will slow everyone down. That requires a penalty stroke!

12. When making a second shot (Mulligan), walk around the tee before approaching it again; otherwise, the second shot will mirror the first.
13. If you want to miss the tree with your shot, aim at it!
14. It is not how you drive, but how you arrive!
15. The goal is to be on the fairway, then the green, then the hole, not how far you can hit it.
16. If you hear glass after you drive, put your club away quickly, look around innocently, and take out your checkbook .
17. Try to hit the ball where you can find it!

BETTER LUCKY THAN GOOD

Who hasn't stepped up to the ball knowing that a good shot is important to have a good game and hit that worm burner? After a few expletives, the screaming ball sizzles along the ground and keeps going up to and on the green within putting distance. Later in the round, the stressful shot over water finds itself hitting the water only to have divine grace and skip out onto the fairway.

On the next tee box, a terrible tee shot flies toward the plethora of rocks, bounces around, and ends up on the fairway. Later, you are hitting over a sand bunker onto the green, but the shot goes directly into the bunker only to bounce out the other side one foot from the hole.

Of course, the opposite results can happen as well because the golf gods are either with you or against you. There is the worm burner that stops a few feet from you. Other interesting shots may have the explanation:

I topped it!

the sun got in my eyes,

it is too hot to play,

it is too cold to play,

it is too humid to play well,

a bug just landed on my golf ball,

someone coughed or talked during my swing,

these are new clubs or shoes or glasses,

I thought the fairway went in the other direction,

these clubs are too old,

I didn't get enough sleep,

I got too much sleep,

I did not eat breakfast,

I overate,

My glove is bad.

Always have a good excuse ready, as it never is your skill set at fault. We are seniors! Swing, swear, look for the ball, and repeat.

It is always better to be lucky than good! I have heard that taking special vitamins and memory supplements has an effect on the golf gods, but I have not found the exact recipe yet. I have learned that for each shot that goes awry, the answer may be, "Keep your head down!" It is more likely that the golf gods are not shining, but it is almost always appropriate to shout about one's head. Just remember in senior golf: *it is always better to be lucky than good! This is the game of golf, not the work of golf.*

MANNERS

I have always said that standing in a ski lift line is the best test of patience. You simply must wait your turn, as there is no alternative. In a similar fashion, on a golf course, the pace of play may be determined by the group in front of you or the group in front of them. It is easy to lose it, temper-wise, when the group in front is golfing from the "wrong tee box" and takes three shots to get a hundred yards onto the fairway. There is a mad desire to hit into them, don't! Anger on the golf course must be leveled at the ball, occasionally at the club, but not at any person. Golf is a game of manners but don't get carried away with that. If someone does hit into you and there is no injury involved, simply place their ball on a tee where it landed. That is a teaching moment!

However, out of frustration on how slow the round has gone or how slow the group in front is moving, there may be a desire to hit before the group is far away. You know you cannot hit them. You have never hit a ball that far until now. It is inevitable at that time that you will hit your best shot ever right into the area of the pokey golfers. That may result in warfare! Have your apologies rehearsed ahead of time, as you will need them!

When catching the slow golfers at the next tee, you may want to ask them if the group in front of them is as slow as the group in front of us. They will either laugh or storm you!

Looking for lost balls slows the game down. Have enough balls with you that losing one or six makes no difference. Look a bit, then move along so that no one can accuse you of slowing them down. It is helpful to follow your partner's ball to help with location. Remember, under these rules, there is no penalty for dropping the ball somewhere around where you lost your original ball but certainly on the fairway.

Throwing a golf club is a no-no. Even though we all recognize the club is at fault, you may injure someone else with the act, so simply replace the club and do not use it again until the next round.

Always be generous with compliments to your golfing buddies. There must always be something good to say, even with the worst shots. Examples may include comments about colorful socks or a nice hat. Even that ten-yard drive can be pretty (maybe pretty awful). Nice putt, sorry it missed!

Be mindful that drinking and smoking may be offensive to some; therefore, do not share a cart with someone who will be offended by your habits. Four hours riding with someone who is upset with you or wants to talk politics is not fun, and the whole purpose of senior golfing is to have FUN.

In the end, after the round is over, shake hands and state loudly: "That was a fun round! I really enjoyed it!" Then go eat, drink, and be merry! At lunch (or breakfast), brag about everything good that happened, forget all the bad, and enjoy the moment!

Senior golf is about FUN! I guarantee with these rules, there will be FUN!

APPENDIX

Words heard on the golf course following a shot:

> I topped it.
> Great shot.
> Worm burner
> Popped it up.
> F*ck!
> Sh*t!
> Shoot!
> Jesus!
> Damn it!
> I lost it.
> The sun is in my eyes.
> Mulligan
> Crap!.
> That's not what I wanted, but that's what I got.
> Keep your head down!
> Uhhh!
> Oh, my goodness!
> Crud!
> I hit the ground!
> I hit the big ball before the little ball!

ABOUT THE AUTHOR AND ILLUSTRATOR

Randall Schapiro, MD, is a well-known physician pioneering the team approach to Multiple Sclerosis internationally. When it comes to golf, he is a nobody. Now retired from his profession, he explored golfing as a means of relaxation and fun. Realizing that golf can be a very frustrating game for a beginner and/or a ranked amateur, he evolved the *"Rules Of Golf"* to make it more enjoyable for himself and the average senior golfer. Humor, fun, camaraderie, and enjoyment are the basis of Schapiro's Modified Rules of Golf for Seniors.

Tim Gaffney is an artist who began his artistic career after retirement. His "can do" attitude and inquisitive nature led him to learn the basics of how to draw, color, and paint – and then take up illustrating professionally.

www.ingramcontent.com/pod-product-compliance
Lightning Source LLC
LaVergne TN
LVHW022001060526
838201LV00048B/1655